Poodles

by Grace Hansen

Abdo
DOGS
Kids

abdopublishing.com

Published by Abdo Kids, a division of ABDO, P.O. Box 398166, Minneapolis, Minnesota 55439.

Printed in the United States of America, North Mankato, Minnesota.

052016

092016

 THIS BOOK CONTAINS
RECYCLED MATERIALS

Photo Credits: iStock, Shutterstock, Thinkstock

Production Contributors: Teddy Borth, Jennie Forsberg, Grace Hansen

Design Contributors: Dorothy Toth, Laura Mitchell

Cataloging-in-Publication Data

Names: Hansen, Grace, author.

Title: Poodles / by Grace Hansen.

Description: Minneapolis, MN : Abdo Kids, [2017] | Series: Dogs. Set 2 | Includes
    bibliographical references and index.

Identifiers: LCCN 2015959115 | ISBN 9781680805185 (lib. bdg.) |
    ISBN 9781680805741 (ebook) | ISBN 9781680806304 (Read-to-me ebook)

Subjects: LCSH: Poodle (Dog breed)--Juvenile literature.

Classification: DDC 636.753--dc23

LC record available at http://lccn.loc.gov/2015959115

Table of Contents

Poodles 4

Grooming & Exercise 10

Brains & Personality 16

More Facts 22

Glossary 23

Index 24

Abdo Kids Code 24

Poodles

Poodles can look a little **snooty**. But in fact, poodles are very friendly. They are also known for being silly!

4

Poodles come in three sizes. They are standard, miniature, and toy. Standard poodles are the largest. Toy poodles are the smallest.

standard

miniature

toy

7

Poodles have thick, curly coats. Their coats come in many colors. Common colors include apricot, gray, and white.

apricot   **gray**   **white**

9

Grooming & Exercise

Poodles do not shed a lot. However, their curly coats easily become **matted**. They should be trimmed every four to six weeks.

11

Standard poodles tend to be more active. They need to run and play. Having a job to do makes them happy.

All poodles need exercise.

A daily walk is important.

More active games, like

fetch, are fun too!

Brains & Personality

All poodles are very smart.

They are easy to train. They

like learning new tricks!

Poodles do not like being alone for long. They are happiest with their families.

19

Poodles do well with other pets. Most poodles are good with kids. All poodle owners agree that poodles are the best!

21

More Facts

- Poodles are very good swimmers. Poodle comes from the German word *pudeln*, meaning "to splash."

- In France, poodles were known for their hunting abilities. Hunters used them to retrieve ducks from water.

- Poodles are one of the smartest dog breeds.

Glossary

matted – formed into a tangled mass.

snooty – showing the attitude that one is better, smarter, or more important than others.

Index

coat 8, 10

color 8

exercise 12, 14

groom 10

miniature poodle 6

personality 4, 12, 16, 18, 20

play 12, 14

size 6

standard poodle 6, 12

toy poodle 6

train 16

abdokids.com

Use this code to log on to abdokids.com and access crafts, games, videos and more!

Abdo Kids Code:
DPK5185